Sister Anita Parks

W9-CHF-086

Little Blessings

A Child's First Book of Riddles

By Sally Anne Conan

Pictures by Kathy Rogers

PAULIST PRESS
New York / Mahwah, N.J.

Little Blessings

is lovingly dedicated to my

Mother and Dad

Text copyright © 1996 by Sally Anne Conan

All rights reserved. No part of this book may be reproduced or transmitted in any form or by any means, electronic or mechanical, including photocopying, recording or by any information storage and retrieval system without permission in writing from the Publisher.

Library of Congress Cataloging-in-Publication Data

Conan, Sally Anne.
  Little blessings : a child's first book of riddles / by Sally Anne Conan : pictures by Kathy Rogers.
      p.   cm.
  Summary: Twelve rhyming riddles describe some of the little blessings in God's world.
  ISBN 0-8091-6632-1
  1. Riddles, Juvenile. [1. Riddles.] I. Rogers, Kathy, ill. II. Title.
PN6371.5.C62 1996
818′.5402—dc20   96-23851
                                                            CIP
                                                             AC

Published by Paulist Press
997 Macarthur Boulevard
Mahwah, New Jersey 07430

Printed and bound in the
United States of America

Read the Riddles.
The Clues Are Fun.
Guess the Little Blessing
When You're Done.

Can't Guess the Riddle?
Don't Despair!
Just Turn the Page—
The Answer Is There.

A Little Puff Tail,
Long Ears That Flip-Flop,
This Little Blessing
Goes Hoppity-Hop.

WHAT IS IT?

A RABBIT

They Live in a Nest.
Wiggly Worms Are a Treat.
These Little Blessings
Say, "Tweet, Tweet, Tweet."

WHAT ARE THEY?

BIRDS

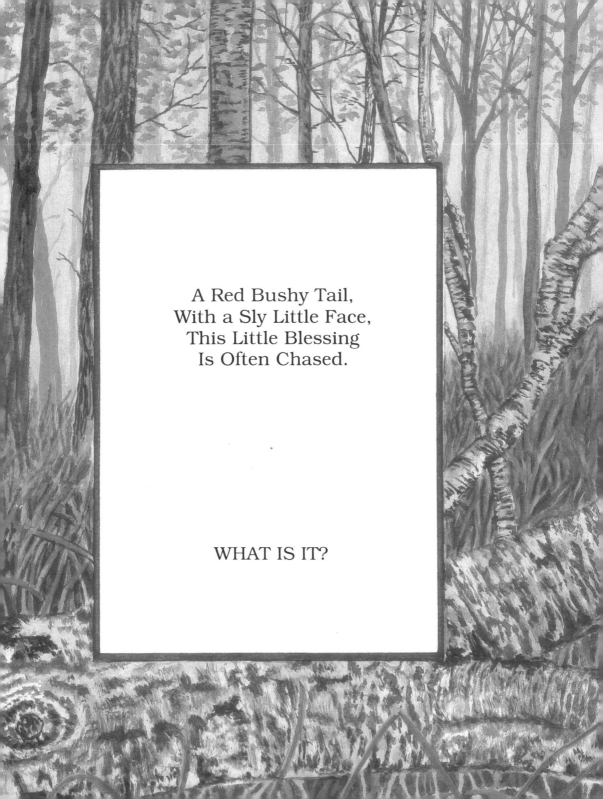

A Red Bushy Tail,
With a Sly Little Face,
This Little Blessing
Is Often Chased.

WHAT IS IT?

A FOX

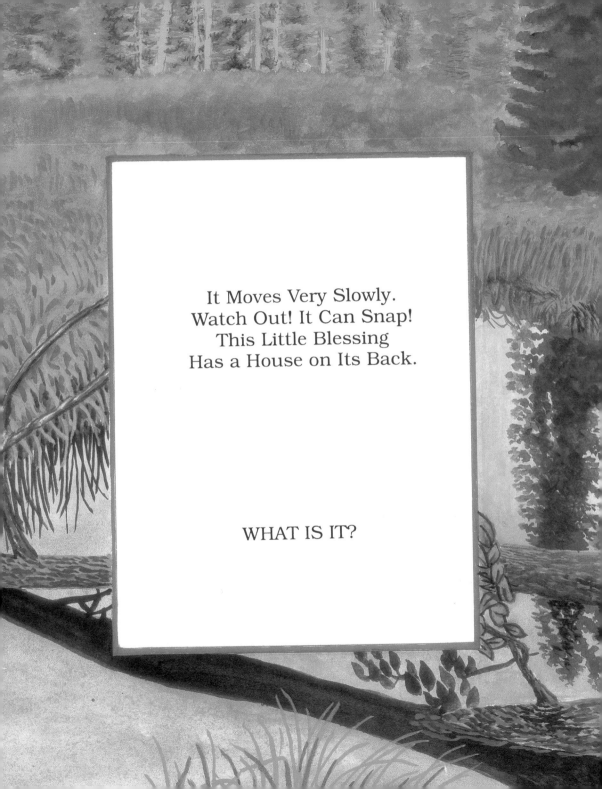

It Moves Very Slowly.
Watch Out! It Can Snap!
This Little Blessing
Has a House on Its Back.

WHAT IS IT?

A TURTLE

When It Finds a Big Nut
It Hides It Away.
This Little Blessing
Might Need It Someday.

WHAT IS IT?

A SQUIRREL

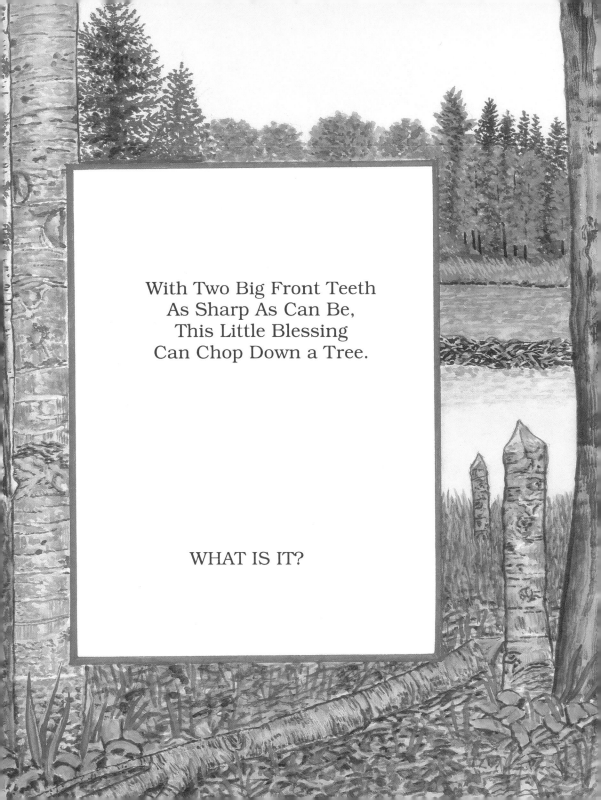

With Two Big Front Teeth
As Sharp As Can Be,
This Little Blessing
Can Chop Down a Tree.

WHAT IS IT?

A BEAVER

It Has Webfeet and Waddles.
Water Runs Off Its Back.
This Little Blessing
Says, "Quackity-Quack."

WHAT IS IT?

A DUCK

It Hangs by Its Tail.
Shh! Don't Make a Sound.
This Little Blessing
Sleeps Upside Down.

WHAT IS IT?

AN OPOSSUM

It Likes Eating Oats
And Apples and Hay.
This Little Blessing
Says, "Neigh, Neigh."

WHAT IS IT?

A HORSE

It's Fuzzy and Crawly,
Then, What a Surprise!
This Little Blessing
Grows Wings and Flies!

WHAT IS IT?

A BUTTERFLY

Sniff, Sniff, Sniff.
It's Easy to Tell
This Little Blessing
From Its Very Bad Smell.

WHAT IS IT?

A SKUNK

It's a Cute Little Bandit.
"Who Are You?" We Ask.
This Little Blessing
Is Wearing a Mask.

WHAT IS IT?

A RACCOON

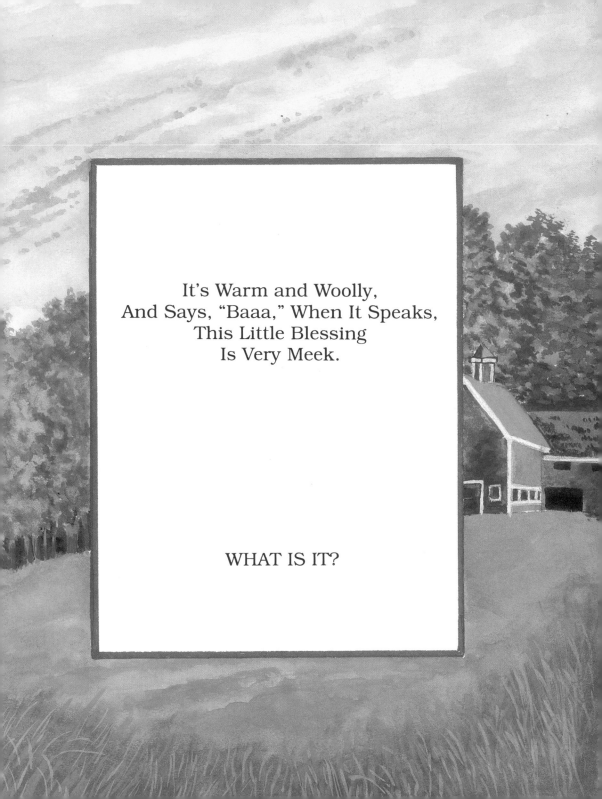

It's Warm and Woolly,
And Says, "Baaa," When It Speaks,
This Little Blessing
Is Very Meek.

WHAT IS IT?

A SHEEP

You've Read the Riddles.
The Answers Were Fun.
See the Marvelous Works
That God Has Done!

Beaver
Birds
Butterfly
Duck
Fox
Horse
Opossum
Rabbit
Raccoon
Sheep
Skunk
Squirrel
Turtle

PSALMS 105:5 *"Remember His Marvelous Works That He Has Done."*
The Living Bible